GW01471603

STUART
CROFT
FOUNDATION

dryden goodwin

dryden goodwin
with essays by sophie howarth and sean cubitt

First published 2003 by Film and Video Umbrella
52 Bermondsey Street London SE1 3UD
Tel: 020 7407 7755
Fax: 020 7407 7766
HTTP://www.fvumbrella.com

film and video umbrella

This publication was supported by the National Lottery through the
Arts Council of England

All rights reserved. No part of this publication may be reproduced in
any form without the prior written permission of the copyright holders

© 2003 Dryden Goodwin
© 2003 Sophie Howarth
© 2003 Sean Cubitt

ISBN 1 904 270042

Edited by Steven Bode
Editorial Assistance by Nina Ernst
Design by Claudia Schenk
Printed and bound in Great Britain

British Library Cataloguing in Publication Data: a CIP record for this
publication is available from the British Library

contents

fugitive intimacy
sophie howarth

Even more beautiful than a laugh is the face preparing for it. I must interrupt. I love the mouth which is about to speak and holds back, the gesture which hesitates between right and left, the recoil before the leap, and the moment before landing, the becoming, the hesitation, the taut spring, the prelude, and even more than all these, the piano being tuned before the overture.[1]

These words were written in 1921 by one of cinema's first theorists, Jean Epstein. It was the lyrical and emotional potential of film which attracted this young poet to the medium and, as this extract suggests, the intensification of experience that could be brought about by its manipulations of space and time. His writings evoke the thrill and intimacy of seeing the world distilled onto screen, and harness all the theatricality of language to draw us into that encounter. Epstein's passionate, romantic sensibility is echoed by Dryden Goodwin, whose films explore humanity through poetic celebrations of ordinariness and individuality, making a similarly direct appeal to the soul. Goodwin's films are full of hesitations, taut springs, and preludes – a relative watching for their loved one to arrive at the airport gate, a man knotting his hands fretfully in a hospital corridor, a football fan waiting with bated breath for his team to score. He focuses on moments of precarious balance and unresolved drama, when time becomes elastic, and the humblest gesture can swell to its full significance. And as we are wrapped in the anticipation that marks his narrative style, he invariably draws us in close. The drama of facial gestures that makes up one sequence of *Wait* (2000) is typical, and Epstein's language provides an apt description:

In close-up, the eyelid with the lashes that you count is a set remodelled by emotion at every instant. Beneath the lid appears the gaze which is the character of the drama and which is even more than a character: it is a person. With imperceptible movements whose religious secret no emotional microscopy has yet been able to reveal, the circle of the iris transcribes a soul. Between a tuft of the chin and the arc of the eyebrows an entire tragedy is won, then lost, is won anew and lost once more. Lips still pressed together, a smile trembles towards off-screen within those wings which is the heart. When the mouth finally opens, joy itself takes wing.

Though a training in life drawing focused his sense of precision, Goodwin's approach to human observation is marked by a rejection of neutrality. The language of intimacy is reflected in the titles of many of his works (*Hold*, *Within*, *Drawn to Know*, *Closer*) and the style of his shooting clearly acknowledges the subjectivity and contingency of perception. His camera follows, traces and caresses its subjects, zooming in close and then withdrawing, as instinctive fascination and respectful restraint compete for control. Sometimes extreme close-ups suggest the camera almost feeling its way across the contours of a stranger's skin, voyeurism giving way to a more haptic visual eroticism. To be sure, Goodwin uses the camera as an investigative tool, but his longing to watch and touch the people he films is characterised by a spirit of tenderness rather than surveillance. The challenge for him has been to find a formal language to express such intimacy.

Terminal 1, Terminal 2, Terminal 3, Long-term parking... Passport Control, Baggage Reclaim, Exit Only... Now Boarding at Gate 54, 82, 88. This is Heathrow, the site of a thirteen minute film Goodwin made in 1994, during his second year at the Slade School of Art. Neither landscape nor portraiture, the film is a study of the condition of an airport, of its simultaneous intensity and vacuity. It opens with an acoustic prelude, a strained electronic reverberation, that acclimatises us to this eerie no man's land. Abstract shapes begin to appear on screen, first blurry and indistinct, then gradually recognisable as lights, grids, neon signs. The roar of an aeroplane cuts into the score, and is followed by fragments of Tannoy information, then moments of elegiac music. As the sound hovers, the screen fills with alternating long shots and close-ups: distant shots of aeroplanes taking off and landing; the panorama of an empty runway; the tip of an aircraft wing; the blurred motif of a tail glimpsed through a lattice of wire fencing. There are snippets of a voice-over, then waves of human traffic, shadowy people hurrying purposefully: up escalators, along corridors, in and out of electric doors. A close-up on the clock... 19.01...19.04...19.10... all within seconds. Everything is suddenly hectic: arrivals, departures, reunions, cancellations. There are tears and embraces, but emotion moves in and out of these transient zones with the immateriality of a ghost, and nothing settles.

Closely related is *Ospedale* (1997), which Goodwin filmed in a provincial general hospital in Treviso, Italy. Here, as in the airport, efficiency and emotion rub up against one another in an uneasy equilibrium. But in this work, Goodwin's camera is more unsteady, as if sensitised to context where life is palpably more fragile. *Ospedale* is also a montage of fragments – close-ups of lips, cheeks, ears, hands; flashes of x-rays and CT scans; snatches of speech: 'very difficult', 'not possible', 'quick, quick', 'sick, sick, sick, sick'. In sanitised corridors, time stretches out unbearably for those who are waiting, while staff move about frantically with barely a moment to spare. Drips are fixed, blood is pumped, a new-born baby is washed. We glimpse major surgery through the curtains of pale green theatre gowns, then an operating table being cleared, and a post-mortem completed. 'Maybe patients don't want to know the truth,' a doctor tells Goodwin. He is there, of course, not only filming, but also listening, watching and talking to the patients and staff. He allows us to sense how bewildered he is by the intensity of so much human life all caught up in this one place, and how absorbed he is by every detail. There are nightmare sequences in which he races with the camera down seemingly infinite passage-ways or points it up through endless storeys of spiralling staircases. There are shots of hands wrought with anxiety or gnarled by age. But above all, there are moments of joy, as the camera lingers on the smiles, tears, and myriad other gestures of human love and support.

Between *Heathrow* and *Ospedale*, Goodwin made *Hold* (1996), a film which, in his own words, is 'four and a half minutes long with a cast of more than five thousand'. As with *Heathrow*, the film begins just with sound, a single reverberating tone that is literally 'held'. Then the barrage of images begins, a different portrait in every frame creating a flicker sequence. Mothers, children, business-men, tourists, people from all walks of life pass by, each heading in a different direction, and each imbued with an exaggerated sense of purposefulness because of the speed at which they come and go. Like the fleeting figures in Giacometti's figure-landscapes, these people know nothing of one another, but their collective separation forms an eloquent composition.

Hold was the earliest work to make an explicit feature of Goodwin's interest in the structural qualities of film, the fact that it consists of individual frames, and that the speed at which these are projected is key to its visual effect. This particular work is projected at 18 frames per second, less than the standard 24 at which the individual frames would have been rendered indecipherable. At 18 fps we are able to feel the full impact of the film's visual assault, its barrage of images replicating the intoxication of urban experience. There are moments of *déja-vu*, when we think we see someone for the second time. But when we try to grasp this, the image we want to hold onto has already slipped away. The impact of *Hold* comes from the fact that it keeps its subjects forever out of reach, exaggerating what Raymond Bellour has called the 'unattainability' of film.[3]

Hold was shot partly in Frankfurt, where Goodwin was studying with the structuralist film-maker Peter Kubelka, who is known for his dramatic demonstrations of film's material qualities. Goodwin still cites Kubelka as an important influence and in several works since *Hold* he has continued his explorations of the medium's specificity. *One Thousand, Nine Hundred and Ninety Six* (1996), *One Thousand, Nine Hundred and Ninety Seven* (1997/9) and *One Thousand, Nine Hundred and Ninety Eight* (1998), all take their titles from the year in which they were made but also from total number of frames that makes up each reel. They are Goodwin's most explicitly structural works and their installation makes as much of a feature of the projector and celluloid strip as of the projected image. The last is typical: a 16mm film loop consisting of one thousand, nine hundred and ninety eight individual frames of

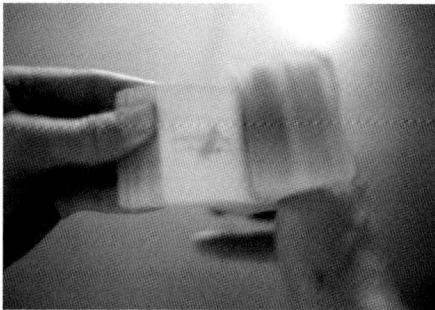

aeroplanes taking off and landing. The screen is placed at an acute angle just above the viewer's head, so that we have to look up to see the planes, originally filmed from a similar viewpoint. The installation of the work explores the shift in scale between the film strip and the projected image: the first reads like text, one slightly differing character following another with colours or shapes recurring in different combinations; the second is altogether more hypnotic, distinctions between images blurring as one after another appears and is immediately replaced.

When it was shown in the exhibition 'SOLO x 9' at Bury House in Clerkenwell, *One Thousand, Nine Hundred and Ninety Eight* was accompanied by two related works, *Suspended Animation – 26 Drawings of the Same Photograph* (1998) and *Drawn from Memory* (1998). The first loops video footage based on drawings of Goodwin looking upwards to watch planes take off in the sky. The effect of looping so many almost identical and almost photorealist drawings is to create an image which hovers between stillness and movement. Positioned at head height across the room from the projection of *One Thousand, Nine Hundred and Ninety Eight*, this work linked the space between the two, adding a human dimension to the experience of watching the planes. *Drawn from Memory* was a tiny flick book that hung from the ceiling in the central space of the installation. It contained a hundred drawings of remembered aeroplanes taking off or landing, and operated as documentation of the psychological imprint of days spent mesmerised by these mechanical birds. As the exhibition went on, the flick book became progressively more worn out, the images erased by finger marks, just as the memory of the planes themselves would fade in both the artist's and visitors' minds.

Between 1998 and 2000, Goodwin made a number of works in which cyclical structures are used to suggest, retract and reconfigure narrative. *About* (1998), *Within* (1998), *Scene* (1999) and *Wait* (2000) all orchestrate different visual and acoustic sequences to form constellations of urban fragments. Assembled from brief encounters and fleeting sightings, they offer intimate glimpses of individual experiences, but ultimately remind us how little we know about other people's lives.

About combines footage filmed from a barge, a train, a bus and an escalator, with four soundtracks, each a response to the pace and sensation of these different forms of transport. Shown over three screens, there is never a straightforward synchronicity of images or sound. Instead both revolve in different combinations, traces of their moods seeping freely throughout the work. In the sequence of images taken from the barge, the liquidity of water creates a leisurely, drifting atmosphere. Railings or branches often fill the foreground of the screen creating elegant but fleeting visual patterns. As the barge approaches different bridges, their balustrades rise up to fill the screen; then, as it passes underneath, darkness intercedes, until the view emerges again on the other side. We see different people leaning over these bridges – an old man watching the water, a young man pointing something out to his son, two lovers embracing. Other figures walk on the banks of the canal – a child on his bike, a jogger, a birdwatcher. Some wave or smile, acknowledging the camera, others are lost in private thoughts, busy talking on their mobile phones, or just too far away to notice the filming. Just as we become absorbed in these gentle aquatic rhythms, the soundtrack jars, the landscape starts to race and we are catapulted on to the footage taken from a high-speed train. We see a football pitch, a housing estate, a series of railway stations, but in its relentless efficiency the train does not allow the eye to linger and every image is abandoned almost as soon as it is glimpsed. Where individual figures at the canal-side seemed meditative, those waiting on metal benches at soulless train stations seem isolated. And where the black and white footage and grainy film stock created a sense of nostalgia from the barge, from the train it suggests industrial grit and suburban poverty.

Within was also shot in black and white and is also comprised of rotating sequences of sound and imagery but, as its title suggests, it is more about internal than external landscapes. Four screens arranged in a circle just above head height show a total of twenty eight portraits including a middle-aged man waiting for someone to arrive, a woman in a headscarf turning slowly to her right, a young girl looking straight out at the camera. There are no stories here, no beginnings or endings, crises or resolutions. Nothing is spectacular, but everything is captivating, the layout of the installation as well as the lingering camerawork holding us firmly within the psychological drama. Much of the fascination for these ordinary figures comes from the restless movement of Goodwin's camera, constantly losing and regaining focus as it zooms in and pans round their private moments of unidentifiable thought. As Goodwin has commented, it is a very sculptural approach to film portraiture: 'I try to make physical space a malleable matter by cutting through distances using zoom devices and playing with the differences between optical proximity and spatial distance.'[4]

Scene draws on both the theatre of the city and the experience of looking and being looked at anonymously. It is very much a nocturnal film, saturated with neon glow and filled with illicit glimpses through windows to private moments indoors. One passage, filmed from the upper deck of a night bus, takes us through the bay window of a Victorian terraced house, into a large but spare room, where cheap

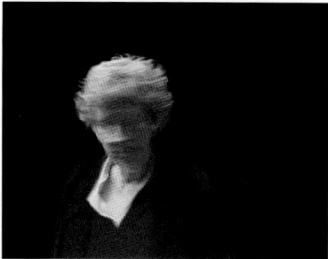

shelving and strung-up fairy lights suggest temporary habitation. It's as if we are doing a quick survey, checking the mood of the interior, looking for evidence of the lives lived there, and the fact that the house is for sale makes this speculative viewing all the more resonant. When *Scene* was staged at night as a life-size projection outside Sheffield's Site Gallery, it both bewildered and fascinated those passing by, offering the tainted pleasures of voyeurism, and kindling the suggestion that a hidden camera might still be in operation. For a time, Goodwin was indeed nearby, recording responses to the site-specific projection from which he produced documentation almost as captivating as the original work. Ostensibly the most intrusive of Goodwin's films, *Scene* finally leaves us with an overriding sense of the inscrutability of urban life. For as the camera peers through window panes, lingering on unheard conversations or hovering over the shadow of a moving figure, the glare of street lights reflects off the glass, affording the spied on an unexpected privacy.

Wait isolates sixteen individual moments, protracts and intensifies them through extensive editing, then combines them with a rousing soundtrack to weave an essay on expectancy that flows and ebbs across five consecutive screens. The images focus on people immersed in states of anticipation: a trader waiting for news of a deal; a woman waiting to toast the millennium; a football fan waiting for his team to score. Each figure is filmed for no more than thirty seconds but the drama of their facial gestures as they anticipate, realise and react to a moment of change, is kneaded into at least six minutes of final footage. The quivering of lips, the welling of eyes, the throbbing of temples; all these tiny movements are exaggerated by the camera as it hovers to and fro across the changing patterns of emotion. The sound too is drawn out, mauled, dissected; in a review Martin Herbert described it as 'a widescreen soundscape driven by depth-charge bass, sudden high-pitched crescendos and reverberating bell-tones which doesn't support the visuals so much as wrench them through a bleak emotional spectrum of its own.' Through these visual and acoustic manipulations, Goodwin attempts to draw us inside each psychological episode, to a place where time is subjective and experience relative.

Absorbed into the angst or joy of these individual moments, we do indeed lose sight of the comparative importance of a groom preparing to make his vows or a member of the paparazzi waiting to get his celebrity snap. Vivid and urgent, these imperative portraits demand our empathy not our objectivity.

Goodwin's most recent works *Closer* (single-screen version, 2001 and three-screen installation, 2002) combine his sustained interest in drawing with his distinctive style of filming. Although both films have a clear origin in earlier works such as *Scene* and *Drawn To Know* (2000) (a series of drawings inscribed over photographic portraits), their methodology is unique. Using a laser pointer Goodwin wandered the night-time streets of central London, tracing around windows with his glowing beam, then zooming in on people behind the glass, marking the contours of their shoulders, cheeks and ears, as if literally touching them with his light.

The single-screen version opens with a barrage of flickering, soft-focus red lights, evoking the artificial glow of a city at night. As this initial abstraction sharpens, a single luminous beam remains, flickering and dancing, both agitated and playful. It comes to rest on a man eating alone in a steak-house, then crawls like an insect across the exterior window of the restaurant before settling on a woman deep in conversation with an unseen companion. Both targets seem unaware of Goodwin's surveillance, protected by distance but also by the reflections of the glass. Still the pointer hovers restlessly, darting across glassy surfaces, penetrating them at will. Inside a fast food chain, where all traces of conviviality have been washed out by the glare of strip lighting, a woman is biting her nails, waiting, it seems, for nothing in particular. And inside an office a man is working late at his desk, while further along this fibreglass labyrinth, an unattended computer screen flashes through reams of indecipherable data. Everywhere light is reflected off different surfaces, so that the image on screen becomes a multitude of layers, merging people, architecture and advertising. The closer the camera zooms in on individual people the more the focus softens and their edges blur. These optical effects work to literalise the sense of human intimacy, collapsing the distance between viewer and viewed.

In the three-screen version there are two moments when the tactility of the laser beam is made explicit: near the beginning when Goodwin declares his presence by filming his own hand seared by the beam as if marked by the stigmata, and later, when a man scratches his ear just where the beam has hovered over it, as if tickled by its flickering touch. Many of the same haunts are revisited in the second film, but the triptych structure allows different screens to be activated at different moments, creating visual echoes and disruptions that evoke more of the perceptual complexities of the city. Occasionally all the screens are synchronised, creating a panorama or arresting the flow of images with a monochrome triptych of red glare. Such shifts between connection and disconnection, orientation and disorientation are exaggerated by the soundtrack which overlays real and electronic sounds, cutting between speeds and rhythms, sharp tones and dull drones, like an orchestra caught in the monotony and tension of a traffic jam.

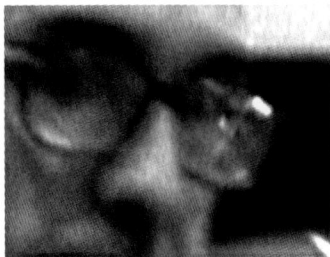

At the beginning of the 'Philosophical Investigations' Wittgenstein considers the significance of pointing by quoting Saint Augustine explaining how he began to learn language: 'When they (my elders) named some object, and accordingly moved towards something, I saw this and I grasped that the thing was called by the sound they uttered when they meant to point it out. Their intention was shown by their bodily movements, as it were the natural language of all peoples; the expression of the face, the play of the eyes, the movement of other parts of the body, and the tone of the voice which expresses our state of mind in seeking, having, rejecting, or avoiding something. Thus, as I heard words repeatedly used in their proper places in various sentences, I gradually learnt to understand what objects they signified; and after I had trained my mouth to form these signs, I used them to express my own desires.'[6]

What is established here is a progression from pointing to speaking, and by implication a hierarchy of language over gesture. But there is also an allusion to the impoverishment of language, a suggestion that it reduces the complexities of our bodily engagement with the world to a set of convenient codes. By insisting on pointing as his means of expression in *Closer*, Goodwin restores a physicality to our experience of looking, and reasserts the richness of gesture. The precision of his laser beam calls for our close attention, but it is not didactic. Rather it invites us to follow, exploring the world with it and through it. Goodwin often comments on the extent to which the viewer of his works is at the forefront of his mind when filming. With the laser beam he seems to have found a way to take the viewer by the hand, showing rather than telling them about the world as he sees it.

And as Goodwin has come closer, both physically and psychologically, to those he films, his aesthetic has come closer to Epstein's concept of *photogenie*. Epstein used the term to describe the way film can capture fleeting fragments of modern experience, too overwhelming and intense to be described in words. Essential to this is a sense of defamiliarisation, a way of restoring the soul to ordinary or apparently insignificant moments. 'Meticulous, deep-seated, dissected, intensified, itemised, applied banality will lend the cinematic drama a startling depth of humanity, an immensely enhanced power of suggestion, an unprecedented emotive force,' Epstein argued.7 And the means he identified for 'maximum expression of this photogenie' was the close-up, whose impact is consummate in the final moments in *Closer* when, one by one, people become aware of Goodwin's camera and return its gaze head on.

> The close-up modifies the drama by the impact of proximity. Pain is within reach. If I stretch out my arm I touch you, and that is intimacy. I can count the eyelashes of this suffering. I would be able to taste the tears. Never before has a face turned to mine in that way. Ever closer it presses against me, and I follow it face to face. It's not even true that there is air between us; I consume it.8

1   Jean Epstein, 'Magnification' (1921), reprinted in Richard Abel (ed.), *French film theory and criticism Vol. 1 1907-29*, London: Princeton University Press 1993 p. 236

2   Jean Epstein, 'For a new Avant-Garde' (1925) reprinted in Abel, p.351

3   See Bellour, 'The Unattainable Text' in *Screen* vol.13, no.3, Autumn 1975

4   Dryden Goodwin interviewed by Akiki Braine in *Slade*, Issue 2, Spring 2002

5   Martin Herbert, review of *Pandaemonium*, *Time Out* 11-18 November 1998

6   Ludwig Wittgenstein, *Philosophical Investigations*, New York: MacMillan 1963, p.4

7   Jean Epstein, 'Art of Incidence' (1927) reprinted in Abel, p.413

8   Jean Epstein, 'Magnification' (1921), reprinted in Abel, p.239

video installations

about
3 screen video installation with soundtrack, 1998, complete sound and visual cycle 54 minutes

within
4 screen video installation with soundtrack, 1998, complete sound and visual cycle 24 minutes

wait
5 screen video installation with soundtrack, 2000, complete sound and visual cycle 48 minutes   **22**

scene
single-screen video installation with soundtrack, 1999, complete sound and visual cycle 70 minutes **24**

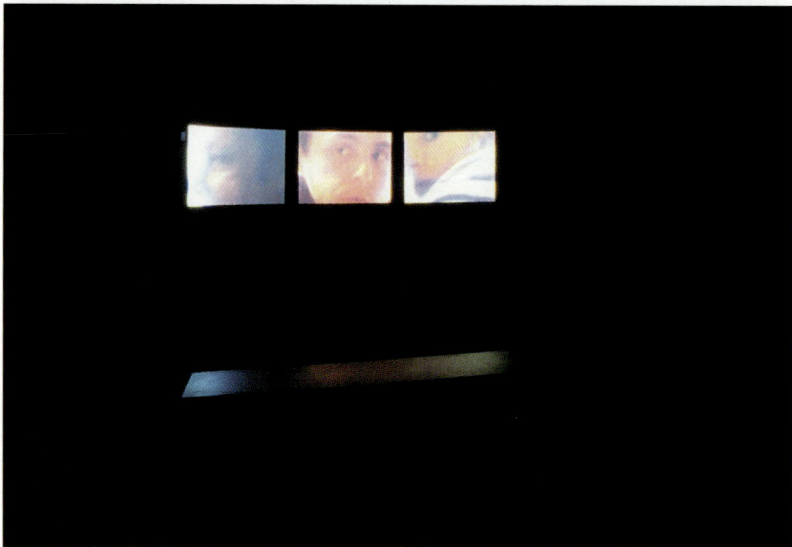

closer (three screen video installation)
3 screen video installation with soundtrack, 2002, 11 minutes 20 seconds

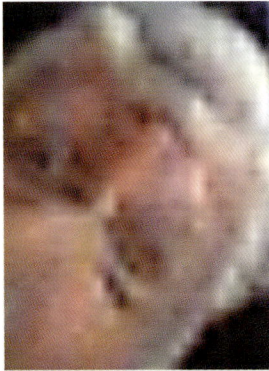

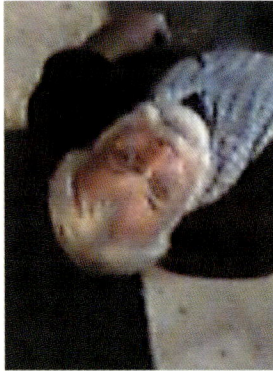

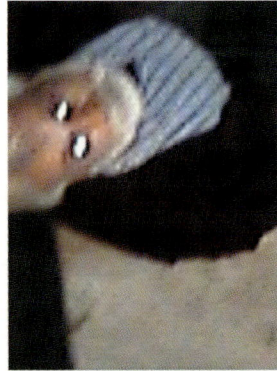

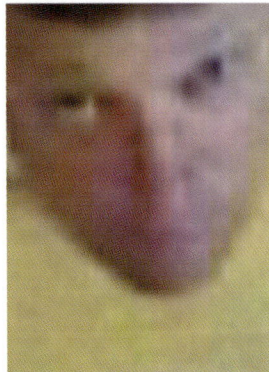

above/below
2 screen video installation with soundtrack, 2003, 12 minutes 40 seconds

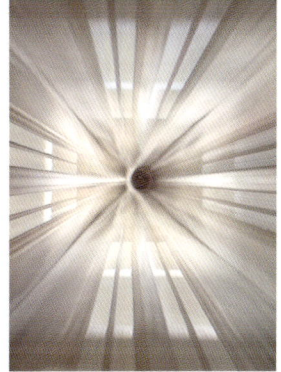

film loop installations

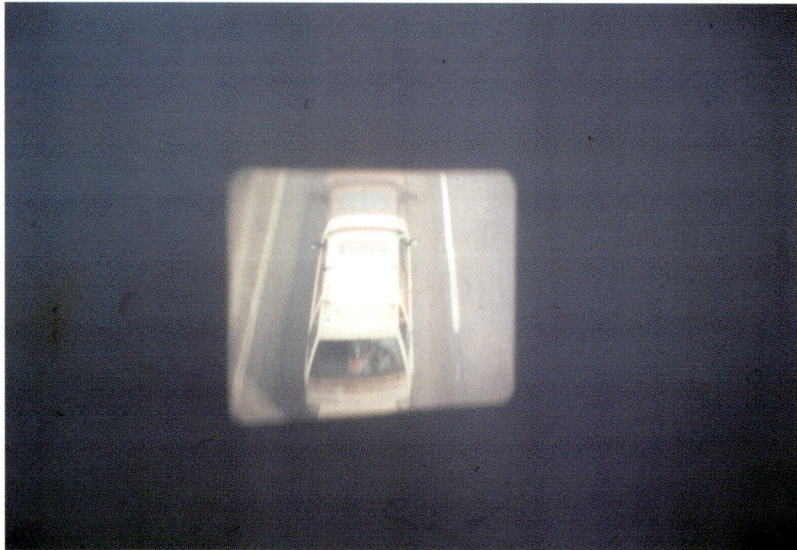

one thousand nine hundred and ninety six
16mm film loop, 1996

one thousand nine hundred and ninety seven

16mm film loop and light box, 1997/1999

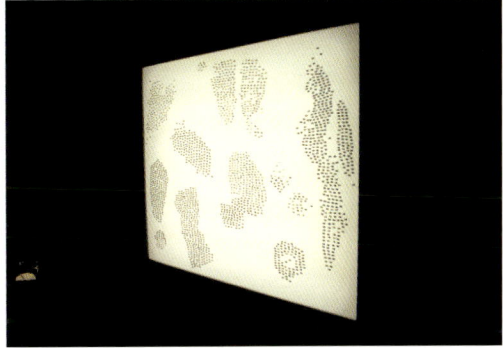

one thousand nine hundred and ninety eight
16mm film loop, 1998

suspended animation - 26 drawings of the same photograph
pencil on paper on video, 1998

drawn from memory
flickbook, pencil on paper, 1998

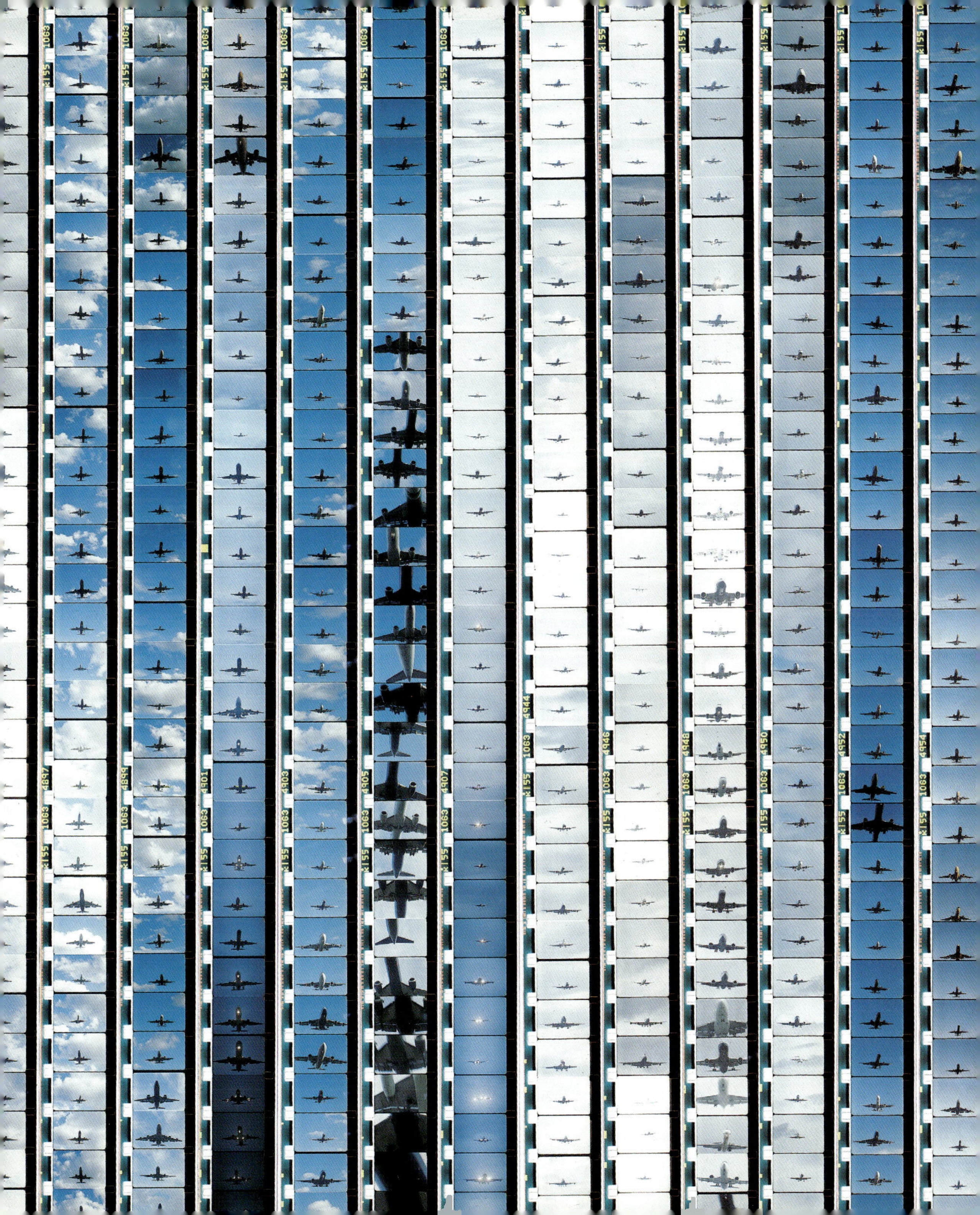

single-screen films

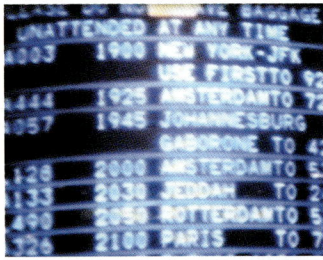

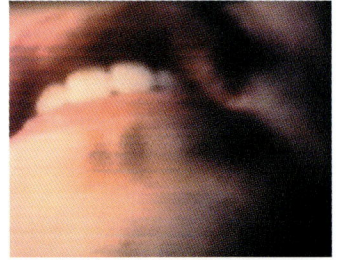

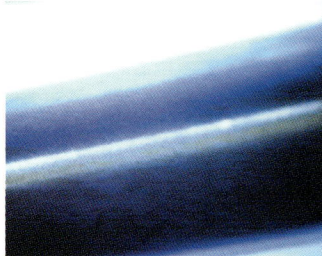

heathrow
13 minutes, 1994

hold
4 minutes 30 seconds, 1996

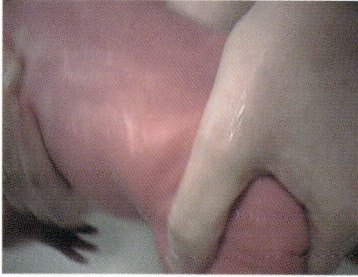

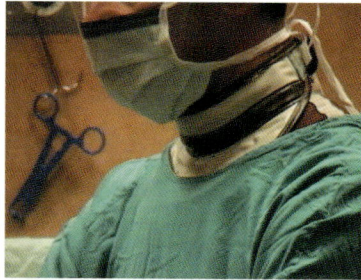

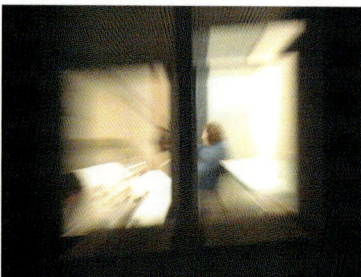

ospedale
17 minutes, 1997

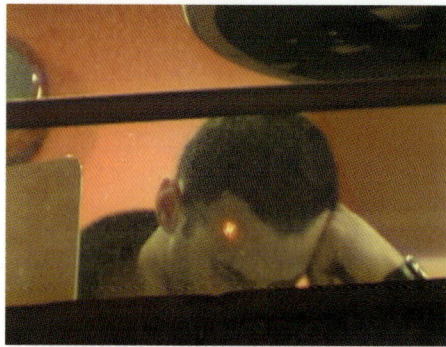

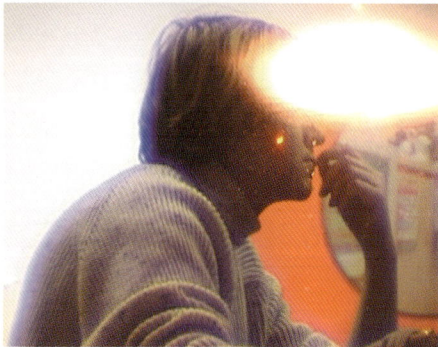

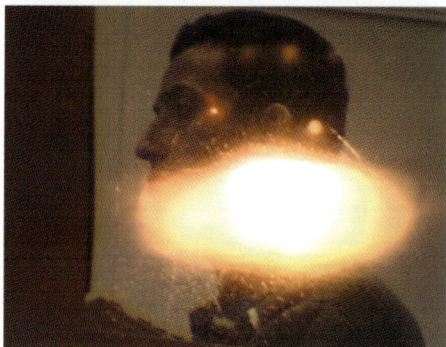

closer (short film)
6 minutes 30 seconds, 2001

Years afterwards, I still remember the woman with the glasses waiting at, where? – an airport? How her face, at rest, as it might be, just waiting, thoughts drifting through, occasionally looking up or about as if remembering why she's there, or checking a noticeboard or looking through the off-screen space to see if whoever it is she's waiting for has come, how her face registers, with the slightest adjustment of a muscle, the range from abandonment to a joy that stretches back her ears and hairline, opening her face. She is one of the figures in *Wait*. I can recall wondering whether she knew she was being filmed, and whether, anyway, she forgot, or whether Goodwin just captured that random face among all the others with a telephoto lens, as would appear from the large blurred silhouettes that traverse the line between her and the camera, and whether maybe she never knew that she was becoming art.

What I had forgotten was how she runs her hands through her hair. It is an ordinary gesture, habitual, banal, but in the slowed-down replay of her motion, how the hair's weight drifts from the suspended screen into the viewing eye. If you've seen the movie 'Final Fantasy', you've seen the opposite: there the animators have worked assiduously to produce a computer-generated image of hair that is as weightless as a pixel. This hair, whose texture is too blurred to define, nonetheless has mass, a kind of drag on the hand that combs it like the drag of paper on a pencil.

That bulk, I think, comes from the sense of time that more and more pervades Goodwin's work. It is not that the work is about time, though for sure in some sense it is. Nor is it entirely that time is a raw material out of which this time-based art is made, though that too is true. It is rather that time, slowed, sectioned, reversed, little by little becomes a physical sense. Goodwin doesn't do those comic tricks with time that make dynamited chimneys rise up from their dust, and he doesn't do the anti-entropic reversals of Christian Marclay or Gary Hill's early work. This isn't about entropy and emergence at all, but about the constitution of a moment in time as a sensory delight, a time fully experienced as time, like the time of waiting, as it becomes a bounded universe that can be inhabited to the full because it has edges and because it is defined by its temporality as a room is defined by its space. In fact, in *Wait*

object lessons
sean cubitt

you can feel the spaces gather about the figures that are observed in it, space being produced, as Henri Lefebvre would say, in this case out of the shape of a waiting that attends to some expected event over there, beyond the frame, that makes this 'here' more truly here.

In some of the early works, the sense is of a lonely, particulate universe of people divided from their fellows – *About*, for example. But with maturity, and most of all with the move into multi-screen observational portraits of anonymous strangers, there comes too the sense of a commonality between these characters locked in their worlds. In *Scene*, thus, each windowed space becomes a cel in an urban database whose connections, obscure as they may be, are nonetheless palpable. Room upon room observed from the upper seats of the bus; a bus whose windows also illuminate and frame the artist, and whose glass also reflects back and intervenes as another window in the frame – the connectivities emerge, gentle as the yellow lamps that demonstrate the shared electric sources of the town. What the figure in the landscape was to the renaissance, the figure in the window is to the urban.

The window, like the video screen, separates. But it also replicates, which is the power of anonymity that made the urban environment so attractive, so secular, and in the end so alienating back in the days of Baudelaire and Simmel. And somehow too the glass window and electric light made of the department store and gin palace a spectacle in which the consumer herself became the commodity on display. Yet now some other mood intervenes, not quite an elegy for the modern city's anonymous commodification but a subtle sense that the prize we have won from all those histories is that privacy no longer severs each from all. Instead, in Goodwin's installations we seem to experience that fantastic daydream of everyone who has walked through a crowd – what if that girl, this man, were the One, the unique person for whom my life was meant? What if the uncertain smile that flickers between two passersby as they negotiate who steps to the left and who to the right were always ready to be the messianic moment of true love? What if the flash of the laser-pointer in *Closer* were the flash of love, the sharply indrawn breath, the *coup-de-foudre*? Point to point, the drawing of light, the giving of light, the isolated network connection that might, suddenly and for once only, make the true connection, and so a place out of the random city and its random frames.

Something I love about *One Thousand Nine Hundred and Ninety Six*: the sense of 'here' here. The commonality of all the vehicles that have been and that will be here, in this exact same spot, each for a fleeting fraction of a second, occupying a grid point on the map that will forever link them, all unknown, to one another. Bill Viola used to talk about a future cult that would worship old CCTV cameras and resurrect their selfless memories of empty parking lots and the drip-feed of people walking across them or starting or parking their cars. Unblinking, unconcerned with form, CCTV is like the last bastion of realism. It cares for its patch of ground as a duty owed, and that patch, under that care, becomes itself, as no un-cared for patch can ever wholly be. The interchangeability of one map cell for another is

denied by this seizure of the repeated but endlessly varied evidence of inhabitance. If once the European mind sacrificed place to space with the invention of the map, this retro-engineering of CCTV makes possible a new mode of place, anonymous but perpetually linking all who pass through it, a sanctity shared and unalienable.

That too is why these windows seem so tender: because they are in some sense, in all the infinite variety their similarity proposes, the same window. Behind the frame, every life is unique, and every life can be substituted for every other. And this is utterly wonderful because it means that the lives beyond those anonymous frames, framed anonymously and unnamed and unidentified, are also in some sense my life. The mere absence of knowledge cannot hide the real capacity for empathy.

And it is this, in the end, or perhaps the beginning, which describes for me the quality of Goodwin's work. Not just his generosity, the affection that he anchors in every face (increasingly so in the more recent work since *Ospedale*) not just the messianic moments of arrival, recognition or refusal. Not even the extraordinary ability to derive from film and video a tactile sense of the sensory presence of palpable humans and haptic surfaces, the uniquely temporal (because temporary) description of touch as something that occupies and perhaps even creates time or whatever word we can use to distinguish a specific duration, like a specific place, from the gridded extension of clock time and map space.

No, this empathy, though it is entirely technical in its working, is not only about an emotion or an intelligence but about a medium. If Goodwin's work is centrally portraiture – and even the abstract effects he derives from re-filming or focus-pulling are portraiture in the sense that they evoke the touch and time of being there – it is also centrally photographic. The video and film footage draws extensively on its photographic heritage, most obviously in the permutations on motion blur that over and again retrace the temporal dimension of even the apparently static instant. Photography pulls at the images, tender but remorseless – the focal length pulls a figure from its ground, while at the same time palpating the ground, taking its pulse more than mapping its geography. Racked out of clarity, the parallax moves of *Scene* have that cubist proclivity for rendering onto the flatness of the screen a sensory account of what dimensionality feels like, emotionally and to the epidermis – how the glow of a lamp warms one side of your face, your tongue feels between your lips, a bay window builds a three-dimensional image of the one who stands in it.

Most of all, however, it is not the photo but the *graphic* at work in these investigations, and in particular those early definitions of photography that described it, in Fox Talbot's famous words, as 'the pencil of nature'. In his 'Short History of Photography', Benjamin discusses the old portraits of the 19th century, how they required the sitter to stay still for some decent length of time, allowing them to think, and to be portrayed thinking. To recapture that sort of depth is the ambition of many art photographers. But where Goodwin is unusual is that he has taken the pencil of nature and drawn with it.

Drawing, life-drawing, belongs to a strange discipline. If today we think, wrongly, that an image is something that exists in a single instant, it is because we have become used to the grid, and to the idea that there is never only one image, but always a river of images rushing by, and that the next, and the next, and the next are always more significant than the one that is already here and now. Schooled in wanting to see what happens next, what's round the corner, where else we can go, there's little store to put in waiting while a single image sifts into consciousness like flour into a bowl. But that of course was what Fox Talbot had in mind; a longer, slower process through which light marked its own portrait on the silver salts, first the brightest patches, then the dimmer, softer, subtler grays. The daguerrotype was not for snapshots but for a process we today would call time-consuming, only because for us time has become a commodity to be consumed, set aside, saved or spent. Drawing with light has a different property – to make time, to create time, to detour time from its regulated course and make it irrigate another field and a slower-growing crop.

Definitionally, as Goodwin's title *Drawn to Know* recalls, drawing as art and act has in its store of memories the drawing of water from a well, the cool draught for the draughtsman and his dray, drawing near. The word was still used for gutting poultry when I was a boy; the act of drawing has its memories of the hands holding flesh, as the repeated frame of a flap of intestinal wall and its beautiful blood vessels held for admiration in *Ospedale* is drawn, taut like a bowstring or the skin over a drum, or your face suddenly embarrassed to be touched by a blind uncle's hand. I think of the elderly Asian woman in *Drawn to Know*, her skin inhabited by time, her own life, yes, but also that life that the artist has handled in the long process of observation, the long lobes of her ears inscribed with what memories we cannot guess, but draughted into the army of the artist's and our recollection, deprived of the specificity of 'my memories' but regathered in the anonymous wisdoms of what 'we' remember, she and I and you and Dryden Goodwin.

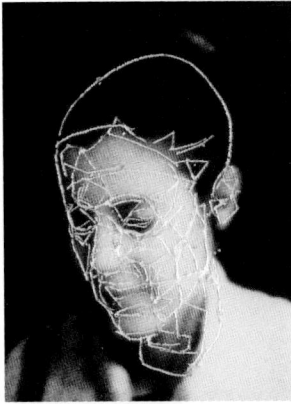

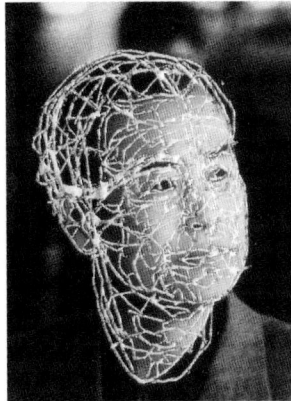

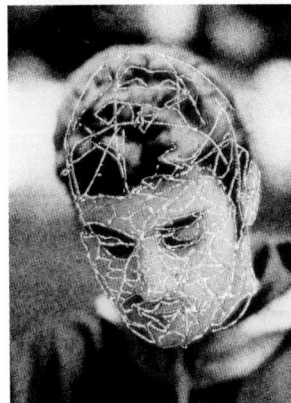

It would be hard to say that these are entirely innocent and exclusively humane collections of images or recollections of memory, or that time as a material and technique for art is all in the doing well, the generosity of heart. On the other hand, to anathematise Goodwin's telephoto as freely as we do those of the paparazzi or condemn so easily in the banal sexism of the movies, advertising and TV would be mistaken too. These images are in some sense drawn from life, extracted from the lives in which they have their fullest meaning: these are not family album portraits, and are often unkind (though rarely if ever cruel). In Goodwin's series of scratched photo portraits, *Cradle*, distance and proximity play on one another as formal movements between attraction and abstraction. How far these are from Giacometti's drawings, the skulls beneath the skin: how cosmic the implication of these imagined structures adhering to the flesh, Platonic ideals meeting the unconsciousness of the line in liberty. These are not voyeurisms, but in another root word of the art of drawing, they have designs upon their objects.

For this, I think, is one of the lessons that these works argue – the necessity of being objects for one another that at once tears us apart and drags us back together again. It is not just that the artist seems to long for company, to reach out with his eyes and craft to huddle with these strangers as for warmth. It is more like that moment in the 'Aesthetic Theory' when Adorno, passionate enemy of individualism, must confront the fact that in our age, individuality is a brutal fact, and any art that denies it cannot use the individual consciousness, as modern artists must, as a focus through which to descry the tragedy of individuation. Just so, it seems to me, Goodwin draws and draws upon the distance between himself and his subjects as on a bitter scar that demands all his healing attention. The tragedy of the individual subject is that, for it, there are six billion individual objects in the human race, and that to be with them is also to know the distances that operate between any one of them and my objected self.

You cannot give yourself to everyone. God knows it is hard enough to give yourself to even one. Nor can everyone give themselves to you. And yet, in some anonymous pact that governs all the sighted, we give ourselves anyway, give ourselves away, like the multiple portraits of *Hold*, any one of which admits to doubt, a flash of arrogance, a moment of panic, an edge of bewilderment. Or in the *Suspended Animations*, the subtly altering modes in which a single person at a single craft can work again and again towards an interpretation, an inscription, of the definitive idea of an object and find it is perpetually other, some step alongside, beside, nearby but never determined or determinable.

To some extent the problems of the late 20th century were the problem of things – commodities, the spectacle, simulation – and the problem of the other – the postcolonial, multicultural, globalising and cyborg-mediated stranger. In the one question of the object, these vapourisations of what once we thought we knew have again a solidity, the solidity that is of materials in which a work can be done, an art made, a reaching out and drawing in, a touching and manipulating. Of course it is not innocent. We left innocence behind us at the gates of Eden with a fiery angel blocking the way. If there is a God, the Talmudic scholars say, He is unknowable. There is only left the effort, however late in the story, to know other people, and to know them not under conditions of our own choosing. No-one said it would be easy.

photography

drawn to know: 12 x people
digitally drawn black and white photographs printed on paper, 2000, 30.8 x 21.8 cm each

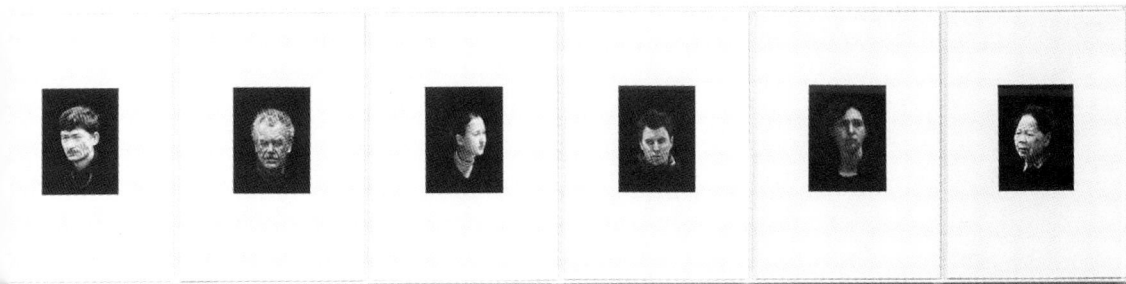

capture - sequence 1
black and white photographs scratched, 2001, 18.5 x 13 cm each

cradle - 1, 2, 3, 4
black and white photographs scratched, 2002, 137 x 101.5cm each

drawing

sustain
pencil drawings with acetate insert, 1999

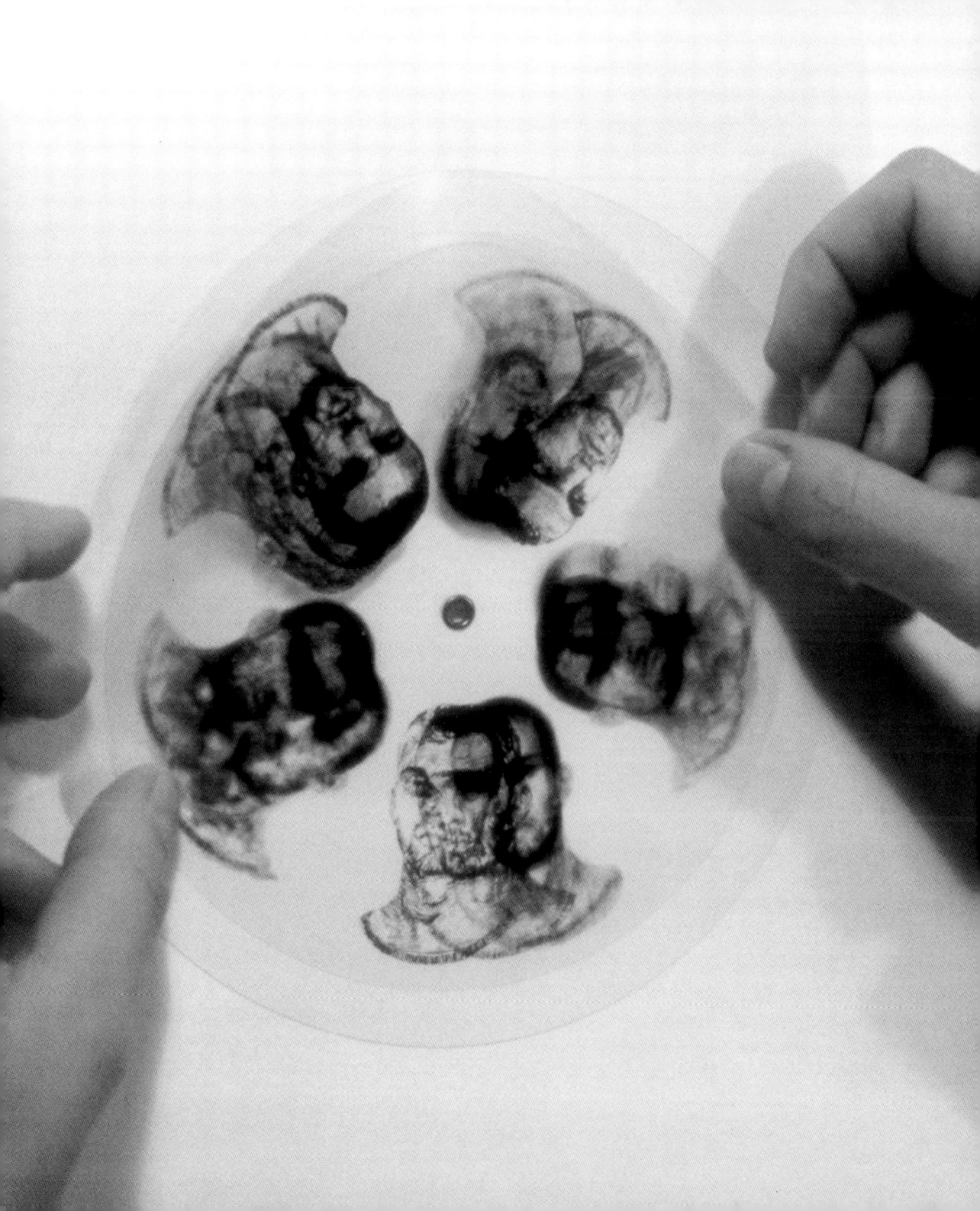

suspended animation
26 drawings of the same photograph

pencil on paper on video, 1998, 23.5 x 17.7 cm each

suspended animation
29 drawings of the same photograph
pencil on paper on video, 2000, 23.5 x 17.7 cm each

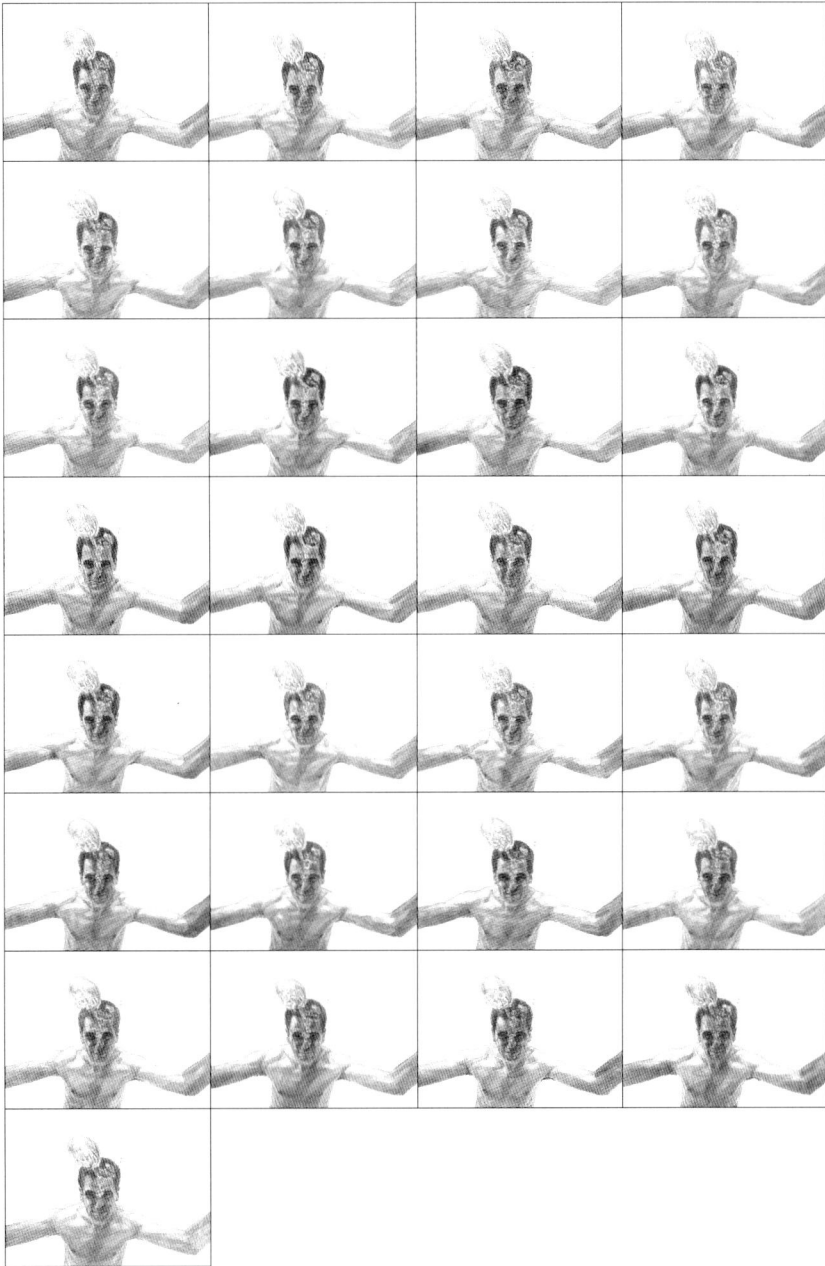

suspended animation
30 drawings of the same photograph
pencil on paper on video, 2002, 23.5 x 17.7 cm each

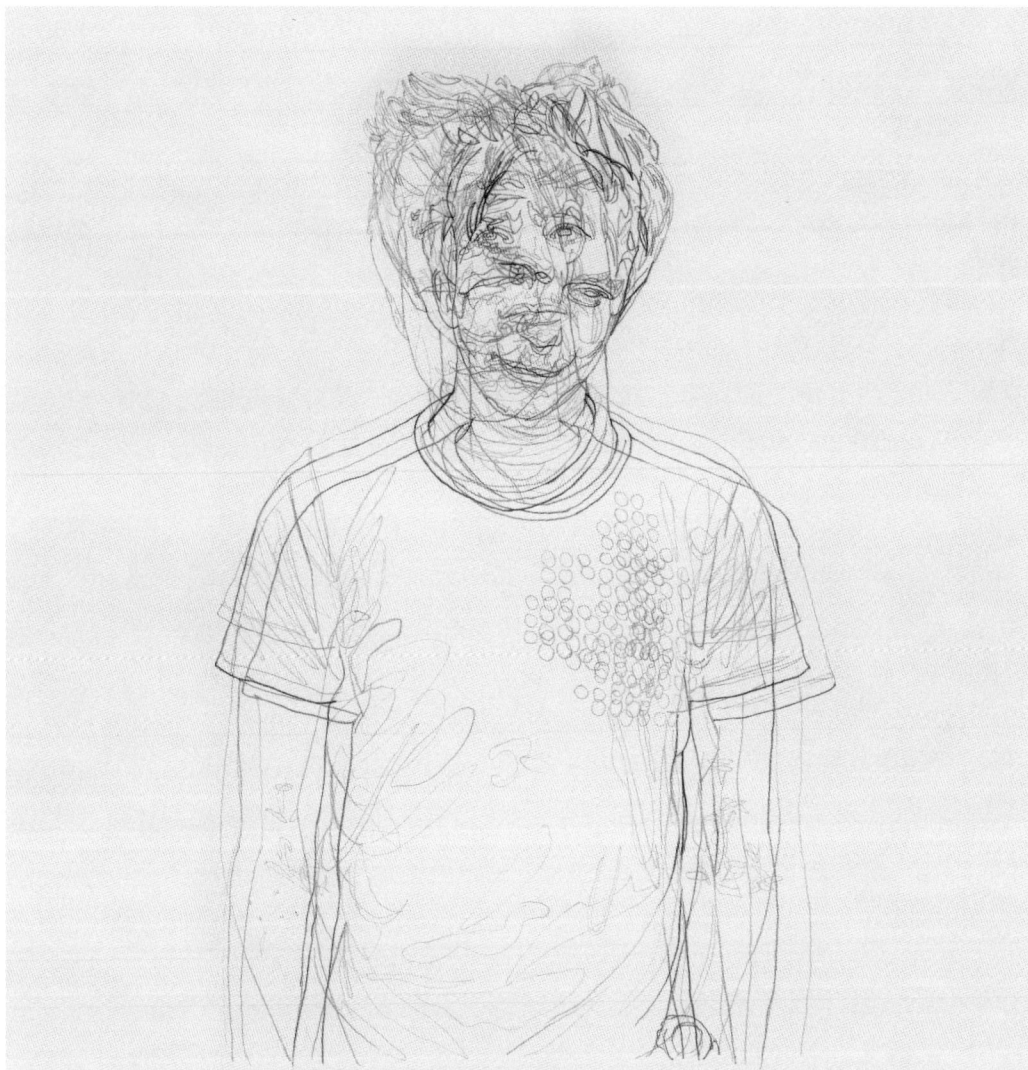

matt
detail, pencil on paper, 2002, 40.6 x 57.2 cm

jeff
detail, pencil on paper, 2001, 136.5 x 101.5 cm

10 minutes →

For:
1. film movement
2. Still & flat panel in relation at the back

? ? ? OVERLAPPING BLACK CITY LIGHTS Could be a dissolve between building dissolve into office building → City

This could be blurred so that I am moving Just one image.

Zoom in then as going in blur out

? change in the sound

Crisp Needenough time

Camera FACEMOT J can use what I already have

About pacing and time don't linger just on one bring them up simultaneously

into single men

Touch man once — then trace in more detail a man?

Should I be tentative and not touch the building then wait till a some point

STILL IMAGE
Crisp

Study building Cacophony

non blurred lots restaurants Socialising different colours neon

Sound people Laughing more passed. Café night intense Piccadilly - no arcade feel soho.

Sound Track then must be lighter Element almost joyful. ie Debussy's - ENIGMA.

Spiritual

Frisson with the touch
An energised moment

monotone. lonely lots of back turned

DON'T USE LIGHT YET.

MAKE AN ATTEMPT

MAKE AN ATTEMPT

INTRO | | | OFFICES | C CENT

① WANDERING DOT | Film with 3 cameras to capture Panorama of image - back in moving hole. | | 3 CAMERA ? | ①
 | | | | ②

② Tableau. City Scape | | | 3 camera / one camera.

③ BUS DOT | | | 3 CAMERA combination with existing ? | after zoom show a series of individuals in offices much further back - then get closer after | ─ Sh
No
S
Ro
En
Ne
wa
Pe
Na

④ CLOSE UP of FACE | | | UTILIZE A REACTION SHOT | POSSIBLE MORE OFF. WORK DECIDE WHICH TYPE DISTANCE/ moving?

ADDITIONAL SHOOTING

up
Sens
disa
Pen
It is
equ
ten

Ne

HAND

ZOOM INTO CITYSCAPE GO TO BLACK ACROSS ALL SCREENS

MAN THROUGH CIRCLE
WOMAN WITH KNEES
MAN ON PHONE

1 second.

Slowly then building to faster
short pacing … more fragmentary

Establish people in different scenarios

…ssed

Light shining

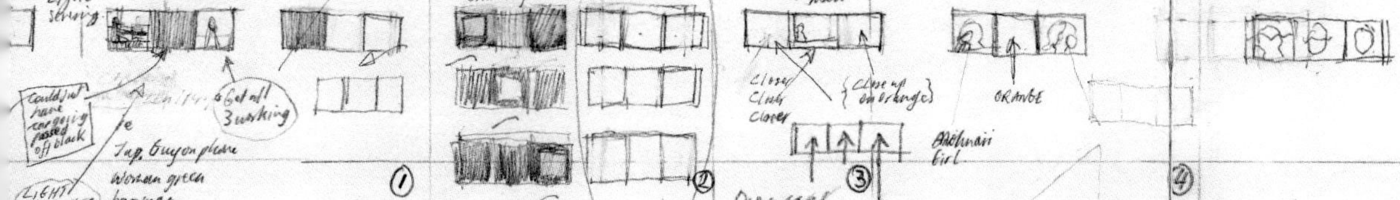

Could just have car going passed off black
Get all 3 working
Closer
Closer
Closer
Close up on orange
ORANGE
Molinari Girl

ie
Jap. Guy on phone
Woman green
barman.
black Guy.
old guy.
etc.

LIGHT FLASHES INTERSPERSED

Lots with Cars going passed.

*Should they have veils over them?

Camera lost in the busyness

(1)

Then.
Carefully more deliberate. down ground. brushing an arm.
Then start touching … fully

(2)

Going from left to right.
Overlapping but not with the drawing

MID GROUND

ie Girl in window

(1) faraway just on building one screen directly yard
(2) faraway simultaneously touching one one after eachother
(3)

Zooming in. Easy everything man.

(3)

DISTANCE INTO PROXIMITY

(1) START with One Moving in.
(2) Then series. fire off in close succession
(play with synchronicity)
(3) More much more synchronized.

MORE DIRECTLY TOUCHING. EASY EVERYTHING.

Bus almost simultaneously

(4)

Breakthrusin.

…dual pace Soho / Picadilly touching …side fragments. Lot of light busyness …e stage you are going to touch things.
Come tom traffic

FURTHER BACK. but feeling they are in the thick of.

3 CAMERA

3 CAMERA COMBINATION WITH EXISTING ?

… lights / activity

PASSED

…SYNESS …nto …

…r BACK ie more distance
…s

(2) …s HALL
…
…RAREA LATINA
…rty
…
…cafe.

(1)
CHINATOWN
BRING OXFORD. STREET
BOARDERS – BOOKSHOP
SHAFTSBURY AVENUE
RESTAURANTS.
HAYMARKET HORSES.
OFF LEICESTER SQUARE.
ie in Arcade Lights NEON – STRAND.
– SOHO –
– PICADILLY CIRCUS / EROS.
– PICADILLY ROAD RA.

…Y MORE …H PEOPLE

TENTATIVE TOUCH

SHOT FURTHER BACK
But more LIKE woman in window

BIG SECTION TO THINK ABOUT!

MOVING CLOSER Touching

SEARCHING AGAIN

…are in the hubbub.
/ Frenetic / Searching
– Person who has had the distance
…ub → that you need to … of
again to start looking / concentrating /

…fferent …

already
WOMAN IN FRAME
OLD MAN.

EASY EVERYTHING GUY
MOLINARI GIRL

*BEAUTIFUL JAP. GIRL
MUCAULEY MCULKIN
CRYING MAN

…side to side / pan. Build up and

lists

Dryden Goodwin
Born 1971
Studied at The Slade School of Fine Art, London
Lives and works in London

RECENT SOLO EXHIBITIONS INCLUDE

2003   *Reveal,* Picture This Moving Image/South West Screen commission, Lacock Abbey
2002   *Closer (three screen video installation)*, Art Now commission, Tate Britain, London
2000   'Dryden Goodwin – *Wait, Drawn to Know*', Stephen Friedman Gallery, London
1999   'Dryden Goodwin – New Work', Galerie Frahm, Copenhagen
        'Dryden Goodwin – Recent Video Work', Mid-Pennine Arts, Burnley
1998   'SOLO X 9: Artists in Clerkenwell', Berry House, London

RECENT GROUP EXHIBITIONS INCLUDE

2003   'The Cathedral', BALTIC Centre for Contemporary Art, Gateshead
        Above/Below, commissioned by Senior Chaplain Canon Bill Hall and the Chaplaincy
        to the Arts and Recreation in North East England
2002/03 'Reality Check – Recent Developments in British Photography and Video',
        international touring exhibition organised by The Photographers' Gallery and The
        British Council, London, curated by Kate Bush and Brett Rogers,
        showing in London, Slovenia, Croatia, Czech Republic, Poland and Romania
2001   'Fantastic Recurrence of Certain Situations', Canal de Isabel II, Madrid,
        organised by The Photographers' Gallery and The British Council, London,
        curated by Kate Bush
2000   'Drawing', Stephen Friedman Gallery, London
        'Video Positive – The Other Side of Zero', Tate Gallery, Liverpool, curated by
        Eddie Berg, Steven Bode, Maria Brewster, Jo McGonigal, Iliyana Nedkova
        Wait, commissioned by FACT – Foundation for Art and Creative Technology
1999   'Video Cult/ures', ZKM, Zentrum für Kunst und Medientechnologie,
        Karlsruhe, curated by Dr Ursula Frohne
        'Traffic', Site Gallery, Sheffield
        Scene, commissioned by Site Gallery, curated by Jeanine Griffin
        'Ikon Touring Exhibition', Birmingham, curated by Alessandro Vincentelli
1998   'Pandaemonium', Lux Gallery, London
        Within, commissioned by Pandaemonium, curated by Gregor Muir
        'Paved With Gold', Kettle's Yard, Cambridge
        About, commissioned by Kettle's Yard, curated by Simon Wallis
        'Real Fiction', Wigmore Fine Art, London, curated by Sotiris Kyriacou
1997   'Pulse', video programme curated by Gillian Wearing, Serpentine Gallery bookshop,
        and Lux Gallery, London
        'New Contemporaries '97', Cornerhouse, Manchester, Camden Arts Centre, London,
        CCA, Glasgow, curated by Hans Ulrich Obrist, Sarat Maharaj and Gillian Wearing

2002	'The Body in Architecture', TU, Delft
	'Mesh', National Museum of Photography, Film and TV, Bradford
	'Commotion', artists' film programme, Arnolfini, Bristol
2001	'Unlimited Edition', Film and Video Umbrella retrospective programme
	Institute of Contemporary Arts, London and tour
	Closer (short film), commissioned by Film and Video Umbrella
	'Canadian/UK Video Exchange 2', Video Graphe, Montreal
	'Video Brazil', Brazil
	'Invideo', Milan
2000	Südwestrundfunk, German TV broadcast
	'Medi@Terra 2000', Athens
	Centre Regional de Cherbourg, Octeville, France
	'UK 99', The British Council, Berlin
	'UK 99', Batofar, Association Signe et Eau, Alfortville, France
	'Canadian/UK Video Exchange 2', Video in Studios, Vancouver and
	Buffalo University, Buffalo
	'Berliner Kulturveranstaltung', Berlin
1999	Universidad de los Andes, Bogota, Colombia
	RAI SAT, Italian TV broadcast
	'Video Formes – Festival of Video Creation', Clermont-Ferrand
	'4 Bienal de Video y Nevo Medios de Santiago 99', Museo de Arte
	Contemporaneo, Santiago, Chile
	'4 Medien+Architektur Biennale Graz – Art Image', Graz
	'Whippet', Stichting Duende Activiteiten, Rotterdam
	'Tram Video', Lyon
	Rotterdam International Film Festival, Rotterdam
	'ROOT Festival', Hull
1998	'Pandaemonium', Lux Cinema, London
	'Canadian/UK Video Exchange 1', Toronto
	'Videonale 8: Internationales Video und Medien Kunst Festival', Bonn
	'Transmedia Festival', Berlin
1997	Melbourne International Film Festival, Australia
	Prize Winner – 'Outstanding Achievement in a Video Production'
	British Short Film Festival, Plaza Cinema, London
1996	Leeds International Film Festival, Leeds
	'Viva 8 – International 8mm Film Festival', London Film Makers Co-op, London
1995	British Short Film Festival, Plaza Cinema, London

CURATED FILM AND VIDEO PROGRAMMES INCLUDE

2002   'Light Structures', originally curated for TranzTech 2001, Toronto
            a programme of work by video and film-makers working in the UK including:
            Mark Lewis, Michelle Williams, George Barber, Michael Maziere, Lee Hassall,
            Maibritt Rangstrup and Dryden Goodwin
            also screened at Tate Britain, London; National Museum of Photography, Film and
            TV, Bradford; Arnolfini, Bristol; Moderna Galeria, Ljubljana

FELLOWSHIPS INCLUDE:

2000–03 NESTA Fellowship, National Endowment for Science, Technology and the Arts
2000   Research Fellow in Video/Digital Media at John Moores University, Liverpool
1996/97 Fabrica Fellowship, Venice

PUBLICATIONS AND CATALOGUES INCLUDE

2002   *Reality Check – Recent Developments in British Photography and Video*, published
            by The British Council
2001   *The Fantastic Recurrence of Certain Situations*, published by The Photographers'
            Gallery and The British Council
2000   *The Other Side of Zero – Video Positive 2000*, published by FACT
1999   *Dryden Goodwin – Recent Video Work*, published by Mid Pennine Arts
            Video Cult/ures – Multimedia installations of the 90s, published by ZKM, Karlsruhe
            coil number 8, published by probiscis
            Transcript, Volume 3, Issue 3, published by Duncan of Jordanstone College of Art,
            Dundee
1998   SOLO X 9: *Artists in Clerkenwell*, published by EC Arts and Wigmore Fine Art
            Paved with Gold, published by Kettle's Yard
            Real Fiction, published by Wigmore Fine Art

FOR FURTHER INFORMATION
www.drydengoodwin.com

DRYDEN GOODWIN WOULD LIKE TO THANK
Jo Cole
Stephen Friedman Gallery
NESTA – National Endowment for Science Technology and the Arts

PICTURE CREDIT
pp22: installation photograph, Andy Keate